Night Angler

Night
Angler

POEMS BY

GEFFREY DAVIS

AMERICAN POETS CONTINUUM SERIES, No. 172

BOA Editions, Ltd. ◆ Rochester, NY ◆ 2019

First Edition
19 20 21 22 7 6 5 4 3 2 1

For information about permission to reuse any material from this book, please contact
The Permissions Company at www.permissionscompany.com or e-mail permdude@
gmail.com.

Publications by BOA Editions, Ltd.—a not-for-profit corporation
under section 501 (c) (3) of the United States Internal Revenue
Code—are made possible with funds from a variety of sources,
including public funds from the Literature Program of the Na-
tional Endowment for the Arts; the New York State Council on
the Arts, a state agency; and the County of Monroe, NY. Private
funding sources include the Max and Marian Farash Charitable
Foundation; the Mary S. Mulligan Charitable Trust; the Roches-
ter Area Community Foundation; the Ames-Amzalak Memorial
Trust in memory of Henry Ames, Semon Amzalak, and Dan
Amzalak; and contributions from many individuals nationwide. See Colophon on
page 96 for special individual acknowledgments.

Cover Design: Sandy Knight
Cover Art: Andrew Kilgore
Interior Design and Composition: Richard Foerster
BOA Logo: Mirko

Library of Congress Cataloging-in-Publication Data

Names: Davis, Geffrey M., 1983– author.
Title: Night angler / poems by Geffrey Davis.
Description: First edition. | Rochester, NY : BOA Editions, Ltd., 2019. |
  Series: American poets continuum series ; no. 172 | Includes
  bibliographical references.
Identifiers: LCCN 2018050058 | ISBN 9781942683780 (paperback : alk. paper)
Subjects: LCSH: American poetry—21st century.
Classification: LCC PS3604.A956968 A6 2019 | DDC 811/.6—dc23 LC record
available at https://lccn.loc.gov/2018050058

BOA Editions, Ltd.
250 North Goodman Street, Suite 306
Rochester, NY 14607
www.boaeditions.org
A. Poulin, Jr., Founder (1938–1996)

Contents

I.

II.

III.

because Ramona . . .
because Edwin, Cary, and Nikki . . .
because Lissette . . .
because Carlos, especially . . .

I wake to listen:
A far sea moves in my ear.
—Sylvia Plath

and the great black hole where a moon ago I wanted to drown
it is there I will now fish the malevolent tongue of the night in
its motionless veerition!
—Aimé Césaire

A river . . . has so many things to say that it is hard to know what it says to each of us.
—Norman Maclean

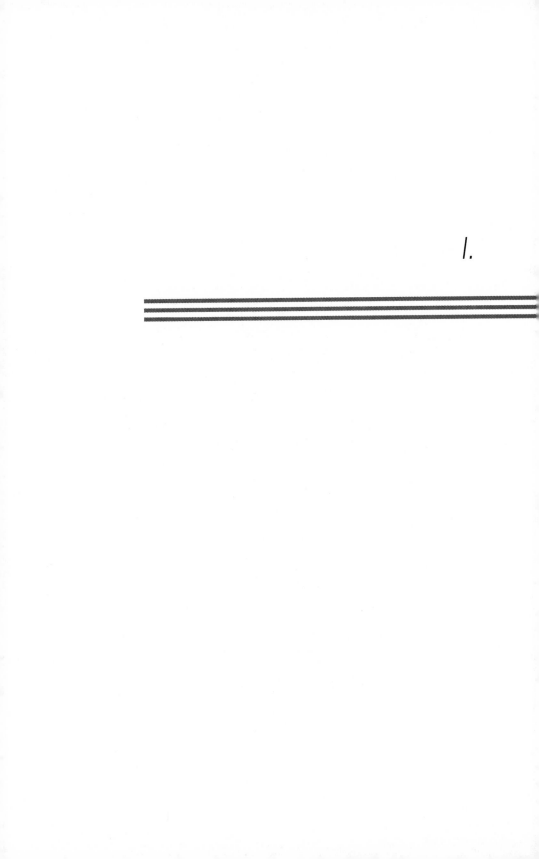

I.

The Fidelity of Water

I.

Thousands of miles from home, you wake
in a cheap hotel with thirst so urgent you have
no choice but to find the bathroom faucet
with your mouth, drink deep, and understand
the daily sigh made by bodies everywhere
in this small town. Your new cushy job gives you

bottled artesian water, which you consider
as you taste the tap. Used to be there was
no good distance between this rivery tang
and your fluid desires. Used to be you'd shove
aside a sweaty friend or jab a sibling
for the first shot at placing lips to the only

neighborhood source. Used to be no future
in yearning.   Feel how far you've come?

II.

Today a flood, and you see the risk
in proximity, in life stretched by loving

both a river and the rain:—to watch what feeds you
run dangerous, the Biblical possibility

of nurture rising into a final rage.
Father rain. Mother river.   When it pours,

and you love when it pours, this river turns
tannic with a turbulence you can recognize

as home—: Mother rain. Father river.
But what course isn't threatened when

the right season licks its lips? What epic
confluence can avoid the violence

of giving and taking such shape? Mother father.
River rain.   If given the chance, you too will empty

or swell—will lay claim to every unrooted thing
in the name of a love you learned from flood.

Hymn or Hum

—for my father

the first time I buried him
in a fist-sized hole

beside the stairs   and almost
immediately he burst out—

bolted like a deer
through the back door

a constant chorus of crows
there have been too many

burials to keep count   some
so small   almost accidental

I don't even notice he's
been banished until he returns

with a piece of something important
to me   carried in his hands:

guitar strings   fly rods   my
son's voice in a fit

of surprise   once I made sure
he was dead—: placed him seven

fears deep and found him
six years later   his bloom

bent and just a little wilted
over a mountain stream

for a while after I felt more
comfortable with him around

heard him as hymn or caught
his hum in the sudden breeze

by now   I have no
choice:—his canny ghost

keeps my son
up at night   rattles the halls

of the house   begging for it
I tell him nothing stays

buried for good   that
he doesn't deserve this

much thought   but really
I want him cast into

the right sleeping garden—:
I imagine he needs real rest

The Radiance

how often will your dearness fly
down the open throat of life

and restart the work of wringing myths
from my mouth   even the promised body

blunders like this   nights I slip
outside as the city sleeps

to spark a sickly flame against the burst
of stars or June fireflies dispersed

in the yard   and then the radiance
of something else awake in the dark

floods the scene   as if to interrupt   as if
your rogue tenderness itself   either way

my head's calamity ignites with conjuring
and banishing—which means I am

a warm diaspora of blues   which means
my hands will fail to carry any one

formula for light   which is to say no
equal signs flare inside this heart

The Night Angler

—for J

A headlamp guides me through October
cornfields, along the slender crossties

of bridges   bulky in waders, I sidestep
thick brier, patches of poison ivy,

all the way to the river's edge, where I kill
the lamp, and soon the moon's blue albedo is

enough to enter water with dream-
fish prowling the currents.   I begin casting

toward the far, cloaked bank: all ear,
all fixed on the grim swish of my streamer

threshing back and forth—a mad bat parting
night air.   In time I will lead my own boy

into the precision of this contraction
inside the throat   this animal alarum in the dark.

When my first cast conjures nothing—
no monster trout panicking the line—

I slide further into the river's cold, send more
barbed asking through deep shadow. I labor long

to lure a sudden swallow—: the wilderness of hunger
pulsing on the other end of these hands.

Bop: No More Your Mirror | *Side A: My Son's Prelude*

—after F. Douglas Brown

When I refused the first watery light
Pooled beyond the birth canal, the doctor
Knifed a second full sky against the dark-
Wet comfort of my mother's *tower of organs.*
For a time that will always seem too long
To her, I made no sound—: Only light.

      You'll never know, Dear . . .

Since then, a harsh history of sound:—
Sharp sonic feedback. They say, "Good morning,"
And I flinch, cup two palms of ocean around
The inlet at my ears—fasten shut these unspoken eyes.
They sing, "Good night" and "You are my sun-
Shine," and I shush them through these ceremonies
Of day—even the ripest noise—: no amount
Of care can soften this clenched listening.

      You'll never know, Dear . . .

The body executes while the eye judges. Because we need
This approach all the same, I watch them
Adjust to my aural fist. They say more with less
Mouth. They begin to see what I refuse to reflect
Or receive:—silted lake:—quiet canary. *This body*
Executes and I will judge and jury and jury until they get it right.

      You'll never know, Dear . . .

Survivor

My arms become two battered branches the first time
I reach toward the not yet rankled tenderness of my son's
backside, bound to the pre-gnaw of a soiled diaper.
L lies in our living room, postpartum and pitched
inside the warm depth of her own recovery, body busy
with soothing the glory of its new stitching. How many
darknesses can turn a desire? How many good breaths
to cast one wound from the sky? I open as if breaking
until a sudden and enthusiastic and sunshiny geyser of urine
from my son's penis startles me into the inane proverb
of a laughter you never see coming.   My hands still shake
as I cinch the boy back into the thin cleanliness
of another waiting.   And, yes, eventually I weep—:
but only after, and only outside, kneeling in the garden,
well beyond the indivisible light of his future. Amen.

First Blood

The first blood drawn   I drew:—
clipped too close, the fragile bed

of the baby's fingernail opened a new red
song inside my throat. When I tell you

I wept at so little loss   and fear
bloomed inside this, I mean

to say I discovered a sudden
window for my waiting,

for paring prayers—:   may what
breaks rise and reach again.

Human Note

We sprawl around this
dumb noise, swooning in its noun-ness

    fact of mouth   den to tongue
electric with animal clatter,

    when the first human note
from our son's mind emerges

    —*hi*—delivering him
across the last question mark

    of his getting here.
Our ears bend to the sound.

The Epistemology of Cheerios

this the week of our son's first
upright wobble from kitchen

to living room   and he begins planting
tiny Os wherever his fleshy fingers

can reach   each first shelf   each chair
cushion   each pair of shoes   he goes

to bury a portion behind the TV
inside the pool of exposed wires

we've been saving him from
since he took to motion   and I let him

go for it   he survives   but why
this risk   how costly this whole-

grain crumb   back from
the wilderness of worry   for whom

Prayer with Miscarriage / Grant Us the Ruined Grounds

Dear Boy: It is true: You took two tries
to get here—for your mother and me
to calyx together a body bold
enough to carry the grace of you. Amen.
So forgive us if we still bow inside
the garden of your miscarried becoming—:

grant us the ruined grounds of the first prayer
fiercer than our cleaved breathing. How could we
rush to rinse the word *loss* from our de-parented mouths?
Remember this: we surrendered a new name
for *everything* to the tender hour at our chest.
Nothing blooms in the old field of *maybe*. No sound

flowers above *please*. But we endure what's not delivered
from the impressions planted by our knees. Amen.

A Proposal from the Previously Divorced

—for L

This ordinary morning in the kitchen, the sky
beyond the window content with clouds—
while half-listening for the sound of you

and our child shining somewhere else in the belly
of this house, I do the dishes to the low hum
of our freshly plucked love, force my fingers

to reach the deep curve of each wine glass,
and spend a full five minutes massaging
the unrelenting corners of the cast-iron skillet

that we—for days—will ignore in soapy water.
I want these careful moments of removing
slightly spoiled meat and filmy bacteria

from the assorted plates of our former lives
to mean all the healthy years I have left—:
which I promise you, this morning and the next.

Pillow Kombat with the Ultimate Sleep Fighter

Those who say they "sleep like a baby"
haven't got one. —found fortune cookie proverb

Like in a video game, size does nothing
to decide advantage:—my demure son
throws his demure weight around our family bed
with resolve, and so I revolve inside discomfort's
orbit, the planet of my sleepiness demoted,
dwarfed—unstudied! Just as I reach my parental

threshold of self-denial, just as I go to reinstate
the matter of physics—*energy* and *force*—he executes
his special move: a combo of lovey words struck
half-consciously across the dark, launching me
into another vain-cycle search for deep space
shut-eye. Then his favorite toy sheep tucked between

my folded arms (**FINISH HIM!**). Then the fresh delicacy
of his foot plopped upon my forehead (**FATALITY**).

Son's Face

my unease no longer flares
inside dreams   mornings

I wake and walk hand-in-
hand with worry—down the hall

to the potty   feel five
little fingers like five pins

on ghost grenades
tugged by memories of the ground

the world can tear from underneath
mixed boys   and I would fall

on each possible
blast   but I need to brush

these baby teeth   and no matter
how dearly I hold

my son's face   no measure
gives up the moment

for each wound I know
on its way—:   in the mirror   we smile

What I Mean When I Say Harmony

dear boy: be the muscle
make music to the bone—risk

that mercurial measure
of contact   there are those

who touch a body and leave it
graceful: be that kind

of wonder   —and if I ever
catch you confusing

a pulse for a path   or a bridge
to beat loneliness   your blood

will be the object of discussion
I will ask to see it back

if only to know the shared sinew
if only to relight your blessing

if only to rekindle the song
carried in your hands

II.

Self-Portrait with Headwaters

My father failed to let our family eat and yet, for years, remained beautiful and resilient to me. Some call it addiction. So now I fear and feign what's spring-fed about hunger, what's dark about my thirst. Run-off watersheds go low and deadly warm for fish, according to shifts in season, but the numbed vein of a spring will bless a river's biota with refuge only the cold can provide.

◆

Like Carbon Glacier, sometimes what sustains us looks more dingy than dangerous up close. A dirty discharge carves for miles before becoming the scenic Carbon River with its sediment-rich current and chrome salmon fortified through their passage back from the deep obscurity of the Pacific. During my most reckless autumn, I escaped the city and ascended an icy trail to its headwaters, coatless. When I arrived neither cold nor hungry and found an ugliness that did little to quiet my stubborn search for a myth to solve for worry, I returned to the river's singular direction—: everything altered, but nothing complete.

◆

I am the only member of my clan to kill something from the Mississippi, to dangle a barbed question into that legacy:—What portion of this do I wish to be true? With a drainage that begins in northern Minnesota, the River snakes thousands of miles between Rocky and Appalachian Mountains, growing by gathering a part of its fluid force from more than half the US states, before muddying into the delta South. I know: the water that school told us to equate with a low-down, dirty terror has long since been divided and dispelled by the Gulf—so why then, while fishing shores of the Mississippi, do I feel and fear hooking a diaspora of drowned faces?

◆

As a child I would climb into the warm mouth of my parents' bed, trembled by the Sunday sermon, ready to beg away a short life of going left:—sins of the curious son, desires of the greedy goat, accidents of the forgetful brother. By sixteen, after sex, I had discovered too many appetites for which to atone. What could I choose but call the spirit of that first prayer—"Keep me with You"—a false course. Anyway, weren't we designed for dispersal, to be diminished by the grave thirst of the fields that lie below? And who would deny the fertility of certain absences? I do, however, love the glamor of an eddy, its unresolved meander, its agile queering of the current's dumb flow. And I confess my gluttony for the immediate, so give me a break—or a gentler gradient—: a little more time to soak in all this contact falling away. How much worse should I be at confluence? How many blues must be banished to the bleary basin of memory? So it goes. So we go. And we go.

◆

Sundown, with maps and flow charts spread around the living-room floor: *I'm trying to distinguish the river's source from its parts—which should show me how best to approach tomorrow's fishing.* From the couch, L smiles with more permission than gentle teasing, so I continue: *For instance, the Sol Duc collects numerous tributaries before merging with the Bogachiel to become the Quileute—: and then, near La Push, all that gathering loses itself inside the vast Pacific.* L leans over my shoulder, her hair smelling slightly of the lavender wash she uses to bathe our boy's body before bed, her familiar *hmm* buoyed lovingly in the bay of my curiosity. *And although it originates up in the Olympic Mountains, north of the High Divide, a lack of glaciers at stream headwaters keeps its habitat consistent:—and so the Sol Duc is one of few rivers on the Peninsula to support all major species of migratory fish.* Though not an angler, L knows how I long most to hold the elusive steelhead in these coastal hands. Time and again I perform this ceremony—part memory, part prayer—and against what light remains, it occurs to me: *I don't understand the why of my craving to locate the corridors through which the right water passes—to make contact less impossible between bodies otherwise drifting apart.* Once more, I've lingered beyond the body's deep bell for sleep, so L rises into the dark's soft extinction, and I follow—: the comfort of her tired steps sounding within my blind but promised reach.

Self-Portrait as a Dead Black Boy

I.

at thirteen   for a whole dark season
I was lethal with my pellet gun   murdering
minor things that wandered into yard   stalking
the thin woods between our house & the highway—
I picked off any bird squirrel rabbit snake
I could track   if I had two surprised seconds

to explain the meaning of my hands   my instincts
would have been to show you the weapon
to turn   hoping you could see gentleness
poised behind the risk—: so when Tamir Rice
was shot X times: the toy pistol he carried
couldn't have killed anything   big or small

even if he'd tried:—   but of course
as the story goes   that math's all wrong

II.

the law among my friends growing up:
whoever's car had the best sound—assuming
they wasn't in trouble with they mamma—drove
we rode the wheels off of TT's grandma's
burgundy hooptie   because of how
the bass from its speakers trembled the tips

of our hair & slapped our young bodies alive
with a beat—: so when Jordan Davis
was shot X times: his legs & lungs
& aorta pierced—a citizen who hated
the rattle that black folks can make when
they make it out the house:—   all around

America's trespass music fell   even now
a different mood than mine hits my ears   like rain

III.

I made it to twenty-eight without owning
a gun   & then my son burst onto the scene
with thousands of miles between me & my
tribe—so I learned it took just hours to return
loaded & licensed   to conceal a new danger
however   as soon as I felt that dark

weight tucked against my torso   I realized
the mistake—how few & unsafe the scenarios
with me pointing this threat at another
threat to survive—: so now   on my knees
I'm preparing my heart to receive the next shots
until a new divinity forbids one more black body

be burned down according to an imagination that feeds
its godliness with fear as seen through smoke

IV.

in my thirties now   I buy sneakers that don't
slip off my feet & feel older for the fit
on the way home from getting new pairs
we stop at a local farmer's market &
before exiting the vehicle   my boy & I change
into our fresh kicks to feel godly while walking

aisles of shining produce & hand-crafted candles—:
so when Philando Castile was shot X times:
a bullet searing through each year
of his little girl's life in the back seat   I can't
see his shoes in the documentary of this dying
but his body slides in & out of his safety

belt as cop keeps weapon trained:—a dark
star stopping the open question of his window

V.

sometimes a sleeplessness
blesses you: in our shared family bed
I lie awake & hear the steady
sonata of my wife & son's unconscious
breath turning our room into
this shore with a mid-night tidal

music I wouldn't want to live
without—: so when
Eric Garner was denied
air for X seconds: the song
& kin of his lungs flattened
above the city's dirty sidewalk

:—let us pray

VI.

on occasion I weep
while watching the living

brown X of my hand move
across the page: swift &

controlled & sometimes remaining
perfectly still——: so I've written

this poem out in longhand
in the best cursive I can manage

under light that bends into something
soft enough to call healthy

none of which can keep me
alive   no matter the grace

III.

I Have My Father's Hands

The heart has wanted so much from them, so much for them:—a few seasons
strung together without needing to fear the things they've torn down.

No matter that they shade the eyes under a sky that shatters with each tone
of desire. No matter that they received the tongue's forgiveness—

no amount of rain can de-monster their act of punching holes into the living
room walls. No prayer called from above can undo the child's memory

of the bird or them hallelujah-ing its broken body into fire. They've mended
cages long enough to feel everything and nothing perched on the verge

of change. Gentleness urged the dream of two separate touches—:
but they keep burying in the forest the animals they have rescued

from the forest. All this despite love, which begot today and another
window opened onto another autumn morning's view, and so many

brittle things darting in and out of shadow. All this despite despair,
which begot yesterday and the sound a river makes with memory turned

against you, and the many notes that can break a thought into still sharper
shards of thinking. And yet, the old wish—: to build belonging

from the daily stone-grief of family—each slab fitted and refitted
with the gravity of tomorrow, dry-stacked: here a coursing wall, there

a slanted house. The heart swears a form can sing these hands back
their best moments. The heart refuses a knell to sigh with their final relief.

Smolder

    Although I know better, I can still
consider *crack* the god responsible

    for my father's failure to shake anything
but rotten fruit from the smoking tree

    of no-loneliness—: he trailed the miracle
of pyrolysis and forfeited the light

    inside his own name. Damn the subjection
of organic compounds. Damn the numbing

    decomposition. Damn the sweet-sick taste,
as if love. I want *crack* to release

    my fucking father from the flame.
Let us tend to the coldness of his pain.

The Book of Family

I.

for a while   our records remained
intact—because mother boxed them

because cardboard stacked tight
beneath the HUD housing

she could almost afford—
but then also and sometimes

and always our story dissolved inside
the wetted mouth of history:

the period of my father's keepsake
pawning   the year of the flood

the times of leaving town
with only what we could carry

in our arms—:   where's
the family photo of this

II.

our belonging has always been
played in the key of desire

on instruments my father lifted
so well—got us to hand over

the steel strings from our
guitar-hearts   each and every

time   as if it were our own idea
to be without the necessary

music   I know that was a kind
of mercy now—to have

witnessed him strumming
his way out the door's splintered

throat   hooked by the sweet-
sick melody of a yearning

we could not hear straining
our lives just the same

What Make a Man

what kind of wound make a man
set his favorite rooster loose

      on a dying hen   what make the man

snap the neck of that twice-broken bird
before his child's eyes   what make him see

      the bad idea after the fact—what open him

like a storm   what make a man refuse
to ask forgiveness   what make him offer

      the sudden softness of his voice instead

what get the man loaded   what make him choose
to carry the small brightness of his child's body

      through the cold sleeping city   —no—

what make a man decide to drift the roads anyway
so his child stay warm in the front seat

      what make him park the car two blocks away—

what arms filled and humming *you are my sun-
shine* each dark step of the way home

From the Country Notebooks

—after Brigit Pegeen Kelly

I.

Once upon a time, my father was offered a shovel
and ten minutes alone with the prized stallion—*Just don't
kill him.*   Once upon a time, I asked about the apple-
knotted scar on my father's back shoulder, as he dressed
for work: *That's from when Sammy tried to kill me.
Remember?*   Once upon a time, my father accepted a shovel
and the problem of answering violence without loosing
too much blood from Sammy's chestnut body, nervous
in the stable.   Once upon a time, I watched my father dare
to ride Sammy, who had only known breeding—: things
went fine, until his muzzle grazed a live wire that sent him
bucking, first with and then without the weight of my father
perched on his saddled back. Every witness there
broke open into a song called laughter.   Once upon a time,
my father couldn't trust himself to spill just the blood
owed, and so chose torture's slow ember over a quick-
flamed revenge:—for one long week, Sammy submitted
to the pull of hunger, easing his desire through
the narrow stall bars for a mouthful of sweet oats,
and then the shovel's handle came down like lightning
across his beautiful face. My father did this
twice each day, despite the wounded wonder delivered
upon both creatures.   Once, Sammy escaped
and it took a lifetime to corral again the full force
of that gallop—to gather back the spirit and grace
of that temporary, hot-hearted freedom.

II.

My mother said I should not do it,
but all night I turned the horses loose.
The farmhouse slept, the coyotes hunted noisily.
I was a boy then, my chest its own field flowered by restlessness.
How many ropes to corral a herd?
I had none but a stubborn concern with steady hands
and the darkness of the summer wind which moved right through me
the way the coyotes moved through the woods with voices
that seemed to mourn the moonlit limits of this release
and those who had prayed for release before me.
I pulled each horse through the opened barn doors,
all night out into the pasture with little resistance, all night my hands
buried in manes as if I were descending into a new understanding,
all night my path a way toward recovery.
And then carrying its own kind of clemency, against
the tall forest of sharp pines, the morning came,
and inside me was the deep-pitched presence a howl builds
at the lonely center of its bawl, before the throat
remembers again that other sweet mercy, silence.
The light climbed into the pasture.
The coyotes were crying and then were not.
And the pasture was—I could see as I led
the last warm body to field—full of memory and motion.

The Fidelity of Music

It took time and travel to understand
how the word *father* sings to me in all
languages——: I want daddy, but *father-abuser* crosses
the notes or keys I believe have barricaded
the badness of that man. I hear *father-addict*
in the damn silence. Of course, my whole-

hearted hope had no chance, which I should
have known once I learned guitar——the first instrument
I tried to turn against him: riffed *father-liar,*
plucked *father-thief.* But for each piece of music
I make into a door for daddy's return
father-deserter has orchestrated, without warning,

another empty house of Blues.   Do you hear
what it means for me to sing my son to sleep?

The Night Angler

as in—one who stumbles
through the dark house

of his life
to drink   hands hooked

to the glory light of the fridge
my prayers ignited along

Let there be fight and faith
Let this man

through
that begs

to lead the frightened boy
through the longest shadow

for something else
the entire way

as in—I see
his face:

still in me   Lord
teach another to move

the nothing
to be feared

Poem in Which My Son Wakes Crying

—for dead blk boys

when there is no exit wound
 his life matters
when there is only the dream-wound
 his life matters
when I still run with all my panic against his hurt sound
 his life matters
when I wrap his finger's non-wound in the undivided dark
 his life matters
when he has been soothed and I lay him back inside the casket of sleep
 his life matters
when I still linger to watch him rest with all my worry against his calm
 his life matters
when he rises with and into and as if the easy miracle morning
 his life matters
when he smiles bright like no more fires need setting
 his life matters
when he asks to have the bandage removed
 his life matters
when my hands shake too much
 his life matters

Arkansas Aubade

—after "Untitled (Throwblankets)," by Pete Driessen

One grief, all morning—: it finally matters where
in the body we choose to hang
our turn: too high & no emotional

legacy longer than loss throws down
against the laden light. It takes risk
& a bloodier precision to ring the next psalm

from the other side of our survival:—
another venous truth torqued
from the crimson length of memory.

What I Mean When I Say Harmony

—for N

Sister, I want the boldest ballad
for you, as impossible and present as the sky—

which is to say, I want joy to find you
everywhere: the wet mopey-ness of

a Western morning eager with opening
its gray smile upon you. I want the Southern dark

proud to hum another brown tiredness
from your body, hymned by safety. In my dream

of the song, there is always a bridge
under which the word "daddy" passes

far beneath us, knowing not to beg
for anything else, doing no more harm.   Like me,

you too seek the tune that will, for once,
convince this dogged loneliness to drop

our worried hearts from its mouth—:
We are ready and ripe with living.

3:16

Whosoever

from the restaurant bar　　I smile & watch my only begotten sway
before the old musician　　who mirrors my only begotten's sway

& strains to lift his bearded voice above the dining-room din—
they've paid him to play below conversation　　but my only begotten sways

two feet away from his blue guitar　　the grace of it giving him permission
　　　　to push
his song out above the evening chatter　　in fact　　my only begotten's sway

commands all eyes: the customers & young waitresses & old man fixed
even the purposeful darkness of the joint seems lit by my only begotten's
　　　　sway

so strange—: how open to perish we have become　　how freed from
first intent　　how surrendered to believeth only as my begotten sways

3:16

So Loved

fresh from his bath   I clip my son's toenails
& somehow the non-smelly
fact of his washed feet conjures the Jesús

of my youth:——for a child he was giant
& silent   & pungent   & difficult
for school children not to burn

down with their torches of honesty
my poor family only stayed in that poor town
long enough for me to fall for Jesús——

me: already the clumsy collector
of the castoff   my heart's false population
of hurt things rising   during dance class

as kids fled & sniggered   I lingered
in the center of the room until Jesús
& I (the new kid   myself pretty quiet & odd)

remained the only unpaired   each time
the music began   a smile was all
Jesús needed to let loose   & I swear

I could feel his swift shuffle shifting
the boards beneath our feet as his reckless
big-body twirl threatened to yank

my arms from their sockets
those were my earliest denials
of communal pain: the possibility

of looking into eyes ignited & made manic
with belonging—of being dangled
by a danger you don't know how

to release   & I carried that soreness home
like prayer—: to the everlasting scent & size
of Jesús   to the ungainly world of his grace

3:16

For

who hands o-
ver their on-
ly begot-

ten any-
thing to this
white-teethed world

if god so
loved   I nev-
er knew him

3:16

World

would you believe
this mothafucka

at the Latin restaurant
leaned in   then reeled

back & hollered *Ewww*
Daddy stinks!   for all

to hear   I admit
I hadn't showered

since the day before
yesterday   in my

normal absent-minded
kind of way   so he

could have been right
which made me laugh

& made him double
down—he asked to see

my arm   sniffed loud
as hell when I extended it

& this time: *Ewww*
Daddy stinks because he's brown!

:—did I slap the angel
shit out of him   did I joke away

another dark American
wrongness as preschool

play   did I weep so that
the whole room would

let him hug my confusion
have I done any right thing

3:16

Blackout

by god—how come *everlasting*   whosoever
begot not destruction   whosoever
believeth not in loss   who faces & clings not

to the never-happen of loveth   only god
trusts the world eternal so uniquely
only god so dearly & greatly gave up

on trouble   not we who serpent the evil
sentence of faith   not we who get the desert
darkness of some deeds   which of us shall

refuse the wrong Heaven when exposed
or entered by the fatal holiness of living light
& how forever is a savior anyway   for whosoever

returns not to forsaken   whosoever
can offer up a body—something precious
& pulsing—without risking the answer: *perish*

IV.

Like a River

Your foolishness knows no bounds. Burdened by chest waders, you make it fifteen minutes into the longest walk you've ever plotted to cross a river—first cutting away from the water for more distance to fish back from—and, with the full brutality of the midday sun carried on your head, you think you see your mistake. *Fool.*

Half the walk follows a highway with shoulders so skinny you must keep your eyes down—: for fear that your lumber, made awkward and difficult by the weight of fishing gear, might lean you into the steady, speeding traffic. A grasshopper jumps from the low ditch-grass, landing on your sweat-soaked shirt, and you feel comforted by the company. *Fool.*

Soon you've gathered dozens, each step adding to the cloud of grass-hoppers at your feet. Because you cannot break the safety of your downward gaze for long, your mind won't stop playing with its first dark thought. Up ahead, a field hugs the highway, and you can taste the anticipation of plush groundcover relieving an ache that the pavement has already begun to pound into your soles. *Fool.*

The tall field-grass too is filled with grasshoppers, and as they build into a swarm around your neck, you give yourself permission to admit the thought you've been dragging with you for miles: *you bring a plague.* Back on the hard highway, a dead skunk blocks your way, but you choose to track through it (and all other road-kill you encounter) rather than risk another second in waiting for traffic to yield around its stench. With the sharp-sick bitterness of decay stuck in the back of your throat, you are struggling to find somewhere in your mind that isn't dangerous to place what is happening to you. *Fool.*

You arrive at the country road that marks the second half of this horrible hike to the river and feel good for making it this far without crying, and suddenly that sense of success is enough to distance the urge to cry. *Fool.*

You look up and see this road is "Hog Back," and it reminds you of your boy and how he sketched a series of animals, just last month—his most incredible yet. Perched on the back of each creature, he drew variations of a little form he called *baby*: Crocodile and Baby, Wolf and Baby, Raven and Baby. Your favorite was an odd bird—its body stormed with orange chaos, its outstretched wings quivering with their reality of flight, and a yellow stare that made it easy to ignore the small intensity settled near its head. When asked, your boy said "Hog Bird and Baby." Because you let yourself be struck by the beauty of that strangeness, you didn't understand:—he was trying to warn you about me. *Fool.*

Now you cry. *Fool.*

You can say my name if you want to: Loneliness. Loneliness. Loneliness. All the curses you conjure against me, all the pitiful prayers you pitch my way, I will catch in the belly and feed. No amount of irreverence or appeal can rebuke me into banishment. Each ritual and hymn ever invented has come back in my image. I change to fit inside the new mouth. *Fool.*

Whenever a vehicle approaches, you pretend to stare off into the trees so that drivers cannot tell just how undone you've become. Look how easy you are making this for me—: your cowardice cloaking us together in a darkness shared but not seen. *Fool.*

When you decide to hold nothing back, when you aim your despair straight ahead, the vehicles keep passing. You are dragging a fly rod and the weary otherness of your brown body through rural America:—no one slows to identify your pain. *Fool.*

As you finally approach the river, you see the last part of your path is surrounded by terrain too steep for you to descend. Once again, you've misjudged just how far down you believe you must go to escape me. Thirst heightens the plummet to the running water below. You have no choice but to retrace the way you came. Before beginning again, you rest long enough to feel your feet throbbing with the prediction of blood. No one can hear this part of the wound, but I accept its offering just the same and will sip from this silent source for days. *Fool.*

To find courage, you think *This is a poem*. You tell yourself *Don't break 'the you'* and *Let 'the you' take the pen*—as if we have any space between us. I gave you this voice, and you've used it to find me. *Fool*.

Another rogue wave of bravery washes your mind, and my mouth begins to water. Yes, yes: what do you think has sustained me all this time, if not the resiliency of your clan, maintained by your own hands? The problem is, you don't believe that you have any more to give. Where do you think we are headed? *Fool*.

You make it to the river at last, wade across, and wait for that old reprieve to commence—: for the current to do its magic and drift you beyond the fresh, unbearable godliness of my presence. You reach down, splash cold water against the back of your neck. As you cast and calm, I lay myself inside that ease and wait. *Fool*.

Your blistered feet burn for me. You land your first fish, release it, and relax. As the second fish bends your rod to life, you realize your favorite name for me has been *Father*. You decide to call the fish "Father" and sacrifice it to this fact. But when it gets to net, the fish looks pitifully broken by what you assume was a larger thing's hunger holding it between its teeth—: be careful what you wish for. *Fool*.

Choosing to build the precious idea of yourself on the banks of rivers means you courted this flood. You had other options and close your eyes to picture yourself surrounded by dry rock instead of running water. Have you forgotten the grasshoppers already? You carry this with you. *Fool*.

You give up on fishing to quicken the end. Absorbed in the return hike, you're surprised by the distant sound of traffic from the bridge you must cross to leave the river. But suddenly the trail begins to loop and it's clear you've taken another wrong turn—: one more ending rounds into something that, because you cannot fly, threatens to send you back through what you're so desperate to escape. Before the word "please" can empty your chest, you hear the murmur of people up ahead. Locals, they correct your path—a small error—and try to assure you that you don't have far to go. See what a generous god I am? *Fool*.

Though you have yet to admit it, I know: you've been thinking about death again. What stops you is the worry that a fuller version of me waits for you on the other side. Either way, you cannot kill yourself in my name. I desire each shade of defiance cast by your survival. And if you're wondering whether I'll ever be done with you, let me give you a hint—: when you're gone, who will make sure your son is not left alone too long with the violence of my voice, which you sang into his blood? *Fool.*

There will be those who offer relief for what you tell them about our day: "spiritual journey," "panic attack," "heat exhaustion," etc. But you know better than that. You rest and recover until I wake you in the morning light. Trust me. This time you understand—: I am here to scare you, not hurt you, and those are two different things.

V.

From the Suicide Notebooks

I.

Everyone has a poem called mercy. —Katy Richey

mine begins inside a field overcome by wildflowers
& with no one around   or with everyone around

but I am five years old   it begins with my very first
yesterday blooming at the back of my mind:

                                    the moment
memory bore this unfinished box for gathering experience—

for keeping it not quite alive   & singing at the horizon
mine begins with worry   the sweet edge of awareness

growing unbearably sharp—:   it begins by fearing
                                        what would follow awe

II.

The song confronts death. —Nick Cave

the city has been asleep when you tell me
I was done once   I relight your cigarette

inside the wind   & you say it again: I was ready
to walk out into the watery dark of the Sound

& now I need an eternity
to place my ear against the warm hull

of your back   I need more moments
to catch the muffled blood-

machine still knocking away   we can't
hear the truth no mouth can get around

we try teaching ourselves its half-names
all the same   —I try relighting your cigarette

against your going   to keep you with me
in the wind   to have you dry & right

across from me   I want to learn
the minor key that makes you stay

to hear you staying   to trust a voice could
sing grief down   that a mouth could hold

the right grace note against our suffering
—: to hold it   as if some bird

calling the whole-bodied sun   & us
as witness   to train the enormity

of that bird on your windowsill
another morning   to see you again—

The Fidelity of Angles

Longing approaches us by *froms*—: from memory,
from holy irreverence, from time zones apart

where another morning's light creeps
all across a distinct range of mountain,

stunning plateau birds into the original
sweetness of song. We want to understand this—

according to our appetite for pulling
a rare, angular music from the body's

dark cathedral. Or we grow stubborn
for the wild severity of the wind

plying trees. We want the vastness of that
motion, then sleep. We desire so much from more.

What I Mean When I Say Harmony

dear boy: aint nothing
not about bodies

we have more than one
sun   more than one way

to gasp inside the heat
and arms of *praise*

worship the warmth
of each loaded light   let your body

grow *fragile*   an offertory   —sweet—
lick   bite   know the *knot*

of your desire   hold it
in your mouth   let it live

let it split   do not leave this earth
without tasting what passes

between fingers   son
always go deep—: find the seed

in each fruit's *buried* longing
if it is yours   sing it *mine*

Bop: No More Your Mirror | *Side B: My Wife's Fugue*

—for L

The morning after your diagnosis, we don't say *endometrial cancer.* Because we've stayed locked in postcoital knots,

woozy with whispering names for the future, we don't dare blurt *hysterectomy.* And the blessing of never having

to mouth *uterine sarcoma* takes months to memorize.
—: Instead, we weigh the two blue notes held by your uterus.

> *You'll never know, Dear . . .*

Ode to the knifed and hallowed midst of your tomorrow.
Ode to the retired wright well of our son's slow arrival.

Ode to the serosa drift that anointed the pelvic gathering.
Ode to the fertile-bombed bardo of probability.

Ode to the sung and silent afterbirths of loss.
Ode to the ghosts now in our bed.

Ode to your head raised from the wet riddle of hands.
Ode to the bloody almost of everything. Ode to the uterus.

> *You'll never know, Dear . . .*

The morning after your surgery, we don't say *endometrial cancer.* Because we've stayed locked in postcoital knots,

woozy with whispering names for the future, we don't dare blurt *hysterectomy.* And the blessing of never having to mouth *uterine sarcoma* takes a lifetime to memorize.

—: Instead, we weigh the two blue notes held by your uterus.

You'll never know, Dear . . .

Pleasures of Place

You are this kind of wonder in the dark, Dear Boy:
I have spent the evening on our porch, smoking
in quiet complaint, comparing old pleasures of places
I have lived—how we leave behind something vital,
and know the fact once we catch its absence
broadcasted by new towns.

                        Inland Oregon made me
miss the shoreline—the salty endlessness
of the rocks barnacled along Commencement Bay.
Then I despised the low rise of the Allegheny Ridge,
which was another way of remembering the West,
of registering my loss of Mt. Hood, and Mt. Rainier
before that—their constant loom no longer
fixing me from the horizon.

                      And tonight it's the thinness
of these Arkansas fireflies, learning me just how flooded with light
our Pennsylvania yard became.

                    As if on cue, you come
bombing out the backdoor, two flashlights in hand, and run
deep into the August dark, where you invent a dazzling
dance that frames your body in this turning I can't describe.
From beyond an Ozark oak, I know you—:
the erasure of my face lit brilliant by the country
of your presence.

The Epistemology of Growing Pains

tonight our son writhes inside the almost
unbearable   legs gripped by another hurt

we cannot reach—the newest metaphor
for the kind of trouble parenthood keeps

pitting against us: *father* or *mother*
casting care into the everyday chasms

of worry   despite the tender instinct
memory stops me from assuring him

something soft and bright waits
on the other side of this bind

who am I to stay poised at the edge
of his suffering   to merely tell the boy *Growth*

be like this sometimes   who are we
in the morning   the way we embrace

the unburdened light of his body:—
a little larger now and leavened

by one more blood-song
for the marrowed ache and awe of tomorrow

West Virginia Nocturne

One grief, all evening—: I've stumbled
upon another animal merely being
itself and still cuffing me to grace.

This time a bumblebee, black and staggered
above some wet sidewalk litter. When I stop
at what I think is dying

to deny loneliness one more triumph,
I see instead a thing drunk
with discovery—the bee entangled

with blossom after pale, rain-dropped blossom
gathered beneath a dogwood. And suddenly
I receive the cold curves and severe angles

from this morning's difficult dreams
about faith:—certain as light, arriving; certain
as light, dimming to another shadowed wait.

How many strokes of undivided wonder
will have me cross the next border
my hands emptied of questions?

Hear the Light

—at *The Giant Heart (Philadelphia, PA)*

Today the boy won't rest long enough
for me to burn a single metaphor
back to whether precision or

prayer leavens the language I need
cast into the well of our survival. And then
the boy urges my turn to stay

poised on a floor scale while watching 24
chilling cups of hurt-colored liquid spill
into a clear cylinder. The gutted window

to the privacy of blood harbored
in this body thins the daily belief
that no sick imaginary could cut us

full open. And then the boy gawks around
a carousel of animal hearts, fidgets against
his surprise at the lesser of the lion's

carnal engine beside the cow's. Before
I can weigh the unchambered bellows
of hunger, the boy begins to sound

a panel that plays the pulse of each beast.
He doesn't linger with a blood-music; he keeps
mashing buttons at random—from the canary's

constant lift to the cavernous crawl
of the blue whale—until I can't see living
inside a god-rhythm that soothes

this earthly cacophony pleading
toward the dark effort of tomorrow.
By now, I have a strange image for heart

filling my mouth. I'm remembering
the tiny fleshy pyramids my own father
cleaned from sunfish. When they ceased

their tight contractions, I strained
to recognize the heartness in his hand,
sometimes pressing down into the soft

plunge of his palm to witness one
last lunge. This memory dissolves because
the boy dashes off, and then I'm chasing him

through the beating corridors of a giant
vascular room. The way is dim
and narrow—: I'm working hard to keep up.

I'm trying not to lose the boy
inside the heart. But every time I hear the light
of his laughter murmur across another

distance, I breathe into the blessing
his life has kindled from the space between us:—
I think I could survive like this all day.

For the Child's Mole

we won't tell you where it lies, as in time
we might need the minor intimacy
of that secret. just creatures, heavy with hope
& begging against the grave song inside
our living, we have agreed his death is
the one cold chord we refuse to endure

from the sorry endlessness of the blues.
& if ever we fail to bear the rate at which
we feel the world pining for the body
of our boy, we can conjure that mole—the small
brown presence of it tucked where only tenderness
would think to look—& recall when it seemed

nothing about our child could drift beyond
the terrible certainty of love's reach.

The Night Angler

Dear Boy: Despite my return to running water
and migratory moods, I have spent your life

trying to break the feathered wheel of habit
in my voice, to bring you evidence

that I am done revising the seasons of storm—:
the God-cycles of hurt breath.   There I go again . . .

* * *

Dear Boy: I played you the voicemails
my father left years ago and understood then

how my tongue will also travel, will mutate
to find you—will draw whatever blood

it takes to carry the word *father* to your feet.

* * *

Dear Boy: I witnessed the moment
your mother galvanized pain into a water-

way you ran to get here—: forget that
and forfeit the first promise pumped inside

your chest. Cut that and you might as well
spill a sudden bucket of your own blood.

Not a day has passed without the word *woman*
holding you in its mouth:—holy with movement.

* * *

Dear Boy: Let the record show we invented
one another: *family*—a lighted story

set against the shadow and dawn of distances.
When I am gone, hold and heat the vastness

of this creation—:   Don't stop speaking to me.

* * *

Dear Boy: On the second message
my father is saying, *I just had to*

listen to your voice—haven't heard you
in a while. And the tribe in his throat

trembles.   How many gardens have I
abandoned to this grief?

—: For the Son so loved the worry
He gave His only begotten reality

and called the Father back.

* * *

Dear Boy: In the beginning
father was a fear I wanted

to call *love*. For years I waded
heart-deep into that doubt

for a version of my name
I could, with some forgiveness,

cast before your image.
Dear Boy: Here's my hand—

because your arrival has
mended the grave current

of time, in the beginning
I was talking to you.

Notes

Epigraph 1: From "Morning Song" (*Ariel*, 1966).

Epigraph 2: From *Notebook of a Return to the Native Land* (1947).

Epigraph 3: From *A River Runs Through It* (1976).

"Bop: No More Your Mirror | *Side A: My Son's Prelude*": Italicized portions of this poem come from F. Douglas Brown's "Body Stubborn," which appears in his collection *Zero to Three* (U of Georgia P, 2014).

"The Book of Family": HUD refers to the U.S. Department of Housing and Urban Development.

"From the Country Notebooks": The structure of section II follows—in debt and in honor—the poem "The Leaving," from *To the Place of the Trumpets* by Brigit Pegeen Kelly (Yale UP, 1988) (Rest In Power).

"Bop: No More Your Mirror | *Side A: My Wife's Fugue*": Invented by Cave Canem elder Afaa Michael Weaver, the Bop is a form of poetic argument in three movements. Each stanza is followed by a refrain (usually from a song) and each attempts a different engagement with the tension central to the poem.

"Hear the Light": A feature of The Engine of Life exhibit of The Franklin Institute (Philadelphia, PA), the original Giant Heart was built in the 1950s. It was never intended to be a permanent display, but the public's attraction to the 28-foot-wide, 18-foot-high, papier-mâché replica of the human heart led to its permanence. <<https://www.fi.edu/heart-engine-of-life>>

Acknowledgements

My sincere appreciation to the editors who showed early belief in this work through the following publications where poems first appeared, sometimes in different forms and/or under different original titles:

The Academy of American Poets: "The Epistemology of Cheerios," "Hear the Light," and "For the Child's Mole";

At Length: "The Radiance";

Bat City Review: "Arkansas Aubade";

Green Mountains Review: "A Proposal from the Previously Divorced";

The Journal: "Bop: No More Your Mirror | *Side A: My Son's Prelude*," "What Make a Man," and "The Night Angler (II)";

The Massachusetts Review: "The Fidelity of Music";

MiPOesias: "I Have My Father's Hands";

Nashville Review: "Bop: No More Your Mirror | *Side B: My Wife's Fugue*," "3:16 :: So Loved," and "Pleasures of Place";

New England Review: "West Virginia Nocturne";

The New Yorker: "The Fidelity of Water";

Ploughshares (edited by Jennifer Haigh): "Self-Portrait as a Dead Black Boy";

A Poetry Congeries: "The Night Angler (I)," "First Blood," "Human Note," and "Son's Face";

PoetsArtists: "From the Suicide Notebooks";

Raleigh Review: "3:16 :: Whosoever," "The Fidelity of Angles," and "The Epistemology of Growing Pains";

Quarterly West: "Smolder," "From the Country Notebooks," and "Survivor";

The Rumpus: "3:16 :: For," "3:16 :: World," and "3:16 :: Blackout";

San Pedro River Review: "*What I Mean When I Say* Harmony (I)" [Pushcart Prize nomination];

Upstreet: "Hymn or Hum," "*What I Mean When I Say* Harmony (III)," and "Poem in Which My Son Wakes Crying";

Washington Square Review: "*What I Mean When I Say* Harmony (II)";

wildness: "Self-Portrait with Headwaters" [Forward Best Single Poem Prize nomination].

"The Epistemology of Cheerios" appeared in *Poem-a-Day: 365 Poems for Every Occasion* (Academy of American Poets/Abrams Books, 2015). This collection also contains poems published previously in the chapbook *Begotten* (Upper Rubber Boot Books, 2016), written in collaboration with F. Douglas Brown.

Once again, my heartfelt gratitude to Peter Conners and the staff at BOA Editions for your insightful editorial touch and your commitment to both poetry and poet.

Thank you to the University of Arkansas's Fulbright College of Arts & Sciences, especially to my colleagues in the Department of English. And a special shout-out to my people from the MFA Program in Creative Writing & Translation—your support and friendships enriched both the process and the vision of writing this book.

Breath after breath of reverence for Cave Canem. Deep love to the 2014 CC cohort (Group F!) for catalyzing the beginning of this book's heartbeat. And wave after wave of appreciation for the Vermont Studio Center. Deep love to the September 2016 VSC residents for contributing portions of faith and courage to survive this book's ending. Amen.

With a diversity of respect and admiration, I say these names dear: Chris Abani, Rick Barot, Kaveh Bassiri, Sarah Blake, Traci Brimhall, Geoffrey Brock, Mahogany Browne, Tiana Clark, Todd Davis, Oliver de la Paz, Toi Derricotte, John Duval, Cornelius Eady, Safia Elhillo, Chiyuma Elliott, Vievee Francis, Ross Gay, Terrance Hayes, Michael Heffernan, Matthew Henriksen, Angela Jackson, Toni Jensen, Amanda Johnston, Julia Spicher Kasdorf, Dorianne Laux, Nate Marshall, Davis McCombs, Kathy McGregor, Rachel Mennies, Dante Micheaux, Harryette Mullen, Angel Nafis, Morgan Parker, Carl Phillips, Kathy Z. Price, Claudia Rankine, Molly Bess Rector, Katy Richey, John Secreto, Tim Seibles, Charif Shanahan, Patricia Smith, Tracy K. Smith, Lyrae Van Clief-Stefanon, Padma Viswanathan, Tonya Wiley, and Avery R. Young. Amen.

For Robin Becker: I continue to grow from the generosity and the integrity of your guidance—for that I am endlessly thankful. And for Doug Brown: I am stunned by the fortune of having your vision in my life, your voice in my head. Amen.

For James McClure: I feel honored by your steady willingness to wade further into rivers and friendship alike. And for Steve Dally, who casts a world-class wonder over the art of living a good life as carefully as the art of catching a good fish. Amen.

For Lynne Feeley, Jeffrey Gonzalez, and Adam Haley: As always, I live inside worlds of affection for your brilliant selves—*look at you go!* Amen.

For Ramona, Edwin, Cary, and Nikki—the lit and beloved core of my motley tribe: with hope and healing, I offer another contribution to our ongoing song of survival. And for Natalia, Jeff, and Ryan: thank you for blessing us with your living love. Amen.

For Carlos: son, there is no language for the light you create, no music that means the depth of my love for you—but thank you for the chance to live inside the wealth and healthiness of your presence. Amen.

This book does not happen without Lissette: you do the impossible to ground our days in love, our belonging in light. Thank you, mi vida. Amen.

Still somehow, for my father, wherever and whatever you may be in the world. Amen.

And there are others that I am surely forgetting: a place in my heart for you too. Amen.

About the Author

Geffrey Davis is the author of two full-length collections: *Night Angler* (BOA Editions, 2019), winner of the James Laughlin Award from the Academy of American Poets, and *Revising the Storm* (BOA Editions, 2014), winner of the A. Poulin, Jr. Poetry Prize and a Hurston/Wright Legacy Award Finalist. Other honors include the Anne Halley Poetry Prize, the Dogwood Prize in Poetry, the Wabash Prize for Poetry, nominations for the Pushcart Prize, and fellowships from Bread Loaf, Cave Canem, and the Vermont Studio Center. His poems have been published in *Crazyhorse*, *The Massachusetts Review*, *Mississippi Review*, *New England Review*, *New York Times Magazine*, *The New Yorker*, *PBS NewsHour*, *Ploughshares*, and elsewhere. A native of the Pacific Northwest, Davis teaches for the University of Arkansas's MFA Program in Creative Writing & Translation and for The Rainier Writing Workshop low-residency MFA. He also serves as poetry editor for *Iron Horse Literary Review*.

BOA Editions, Ltd., American Poets Continuum Series

Colophon

BOA Editions, Ltd., a not-for-profit publisher of poetry and other literary works, fosters readership and appreciation of contemporary literature. By identifying, cultivating, and publishing both new and established poets and selecting authors of unique literary talent, BOA brings high-quality literature to the public. Support for this effort comes from the sale of its publications, grant funding, and private donations.

◆

The publication of this book is made possible, in part,
by the support of the following individuals:

Anonymous
James Long Hale
Jack & Gail Langerak
Melanie & Ron Martin-Dent
Joe McElveney
Boo Poulin
Deborah Ronnen
Steven O. Russell & Phyllis Rifkin-Russell
William Waddell & Linda Rubel
Michael Waters & Mihaela Moscaliuc